FAMILY WALKS AROUND THE

CONTEN

	INFORMATION & ABBREVIATIONS	2
	INTRODUCTION	3
Walk No 1	HEATH WARREN & LOWER COMMON 4 ½ miles	4
Walk No 2	THE WELSH DRIVE & CASTLE BOTTOM 5 miles	6
Walk No 3	EVERSLEY CROSS & UP GREEN 4 miles	8
Walk No 4	YATELEY COMMON COUNTRY PARK 3 ½ miles	10
Walk No 5	FINCHAMPSTEAD & LONGWATER 4 miles	12
Walk No 6	FINCHAMPSTEAD RIDGES & MOOR GREEN LAKES 4 miles	14
Walk No 7	YATELEY GREEN & BLACKBUSHE 4 miles	18
Walk No 8	MINLEY & HAWLEY LAKE 4 miles	20
Walk No 9	FARLEY HILL & LOWER COMMON 4 ½ miles	22
Walk No 10	FINCHAMPSTEAD & BLACKWATER RIVER 4 ½ miles	24
Walk No 11	COVE BROOK & HAWLEY COMMON 5 ½ miles	26
Walk No 12	BLACKWATER RIVER & BASINGSTOKE CANAL 5 miles	28
LOCATION OF STARTING POINTS AND POINTS OF INTEREST		16/17
POINTS OF INTEREST		30

Published by
ELVETHAM PUBLICATIONS
4 Eversley Drive, Fleet, Hampshire, GU51 1BG
www.elvethampublications.co.uk
elvethampubs@aol.com

FAMILY WALKS SERIES

Family Walks around the Blackwater Valley   2009
ISBN 978-0-9553268-1-3
Family Walks around Hook, Hartley Wintney & Rotherwick   2008
ISBN 978-0-9553268-0-6
Family Walks around Odiham & Beyond   2003
Family Walks around Fleet, Crookham & Crondall   2002
Family Walks around Farnham & the Hampshire Borders   2001

© Elvetham Publications. All rights reserved. No part of this publication may be reproduced in any form or by any means (except short passages for review) without the prior written permission of the publisher.

Great care has been taken to be accurate. The publisher cannot however accept any responsibility for errors which may occur, or their consequences.

The walk descriptions have been checked independently, but changes can occur. **If obstructions or crops on the line of the path are encountered, please contact the Rights of Way Officer asking for the problem to be cleared. Give a map reference if possible.** Contact details are:

The Rights of Way Section, (Hampshire)	Rights of Way Office, (Berkshire)
Hampshire County Council	Wokingham Borough Council
Mottisfont Court,	Countryside Service,
High Street,	Dinton Pastures Country Park,
Winchester,	Davis Street,
Hampshire.	Hurst,
SO23 8ZF	Reading,
	Berkshire.
	RG10 0TH
Telephone: 0845 6035636	Telephone: 0118 934 2016
e-mail: rights.of.way@hants.gov.uk	e-mail:
web site: www.hants.gov.uk/row.htm	publicrightsofway@wokingham.gov.uk
	web site: www.wokingham.gov.uk

ABBREVIATIONS

R	Right	SP	Signpost
RHS	Right hand side	S	Stile, kissing gate or squeeze posts
L	Left	FB	Footbridge
LHS	Left hand side	W	Waymark

INTRODUCTION

This new edition covers twelve circular walks around the Blackwater Valley. It includes all the walks from the previous Family Walks book, which have been revised and updated. The usual format of the walk description and its accompanying map on facing pages is retained. The paragraph numbers correspond to the numbers shown on the maps. Points of Interest seen from the walks are described separately at the end of the book.

Starting points for the walks (where parking should be available) are shown on the map in the centre pages. All of the walks can be started from any point on the walk. Ordnance Survey Explorer Maps 145 and 159 at a scale of 2½ miles to the inch shows all the paths in detail and walkers are encouraged to use this map although those in this book are adequate.

The nearest railway services are at Sandhurst and North Camp stations. Information about public transport may be found at: www.hants.gov.uk/passengertransport, or from Traveline – Telephone number 0845 6035633.

The walks pass close to public houses where refreshments are available for thirsty walkers. Please ask the landlord for his permission if you wish to leave your car in the car park (and remember to use their hospitality). At the time of writing a number of the pubs were either closed for redevelopment or in the process of being sold. If you are relying on them for refreshment it may be advisable to check first.

In dry conditions good walking shoes should suffice, but wellies may be needed in wetter conditions.

Some walks pass close to private houses - please respect the residents' privacy.

We would like to thank those local businesses who have helped to support this series of books by taking out advertising space. We would encourage you to use their services.

We are grateful to Bob Rose for inviting us to update the Family Walks series of books, his encouragement, guidance and support. Our thanks go to Ted Blackman for the sketch maps (based on out of copyright maps and path surveys) and to Judy Dawkins and Alison Calloway for checking the descriptions for us.

Stephen and Pam Turner
June 2009

Cover photograph front: The Blackwater River near Thatchers Ford (by Stephen Turner) – see walk number 9 and Points of Interest.
Cover photograph back: The Authors (by John Turner).

Walk No 1   HEATH WARREN & LOWER COMMON

[4 ½ miles, 2 ¼ hours]

1. Start from Eversley Church. Go through the churchyard and leave it by a gate at the rear. Follow the enclosed footpath, cross a footbridge and through a kissing gate to go along the LH field edge. In the field corner, cross a footbridge, go through a kissing gate and ahead along an enclosed path. Go through two further kissing gates and along a track at the edge of a wood. At the end of a field on your R, cross a track and continue ahead on the track (ignoring side turnings). After 700 yards, just before overhead pylon wires, at a 4-fingered signpost on your L*, turn R on a path through trees and grass passing a gas depot on your R to reach and cross a road with care.

2. Enter Bramshill Plantation (car park on your L). At the signpost, go ahead on the footpath under the pylon wires for almost a mile (ignore way-marked gate on the R after ½ mile). At a crossing track fork half R towards houses and pass the Old Chapel on the L to reach the New Mill Lane near the ford across the River Blackwater to your L.

3. Cross the lane to a metal footpath signpost and a Blackwater Valley Path waymark. Go through a kissing gate along the field edge, cross two paddocks with kissing gates to reach double metal field gates leading into a further paddock. Keep ahead to another kissing gate and a small footbridge. Cross a meadow, go through a kissing gate and along an enclosed path to reach a road.

4. Turn R along The Street; watch traffic, keep on the RH footway. Pass the White Hart and shortly after the entrance to Warbrook House, at the end of the wooden barrier, turn R at footpath signpost and along a path through woods. Pass the football pitch on your L and in due course reach the road by The Lodge.

5. Cross the road carefully and take the tarmac drive to the L of Longreach. Keep ahead on the drive to Lyndridge. When the drive bears R, keep ahead along an enclosed path. Turn L over a footbridge and along the RH field edge to return to Eversley Church.

*Note. To visit Cudbury Clump, turn L at the above mentioned 4-fingered signpost and follow a path through a new plantation and some tall pines to join the Welsh Drive. Cudbury Clump is the low mound on your L by the bridleway signpost.

The White Hart

Telephone: Eversley 01189 732817
(17th Century Inn on the A327)

Real Draught Ales

Fresh Cut Sandwiches

Hot and Cold Snacks Daily

Home-made Country Fare Lunches

Welcoming Log Fire in Winter

Walk No 2   THE WELSH DRIVE & CASTLE BOTTOM

[5 miles, 2 ½ hours]

1. Start from Eversley Church. Go along Church Lane, away from the main road. At some white gates, turn L at a footpath signpost up a track through the woods. At the top of the hill, bear L at a waymark post along a parallel track and at a fork bear L on a track leading to a SAGA pillar in an open space. Turn L along a wide gravel track (the Welsh Drive) to reach and carefully cross a road to a bridleway signpost opposite. Continue on the Welsh Drive to cross the Cooper's Hill road with care.

2. Go through the gap and immediately turn L on the marked bridleway. At a T-junction, turn L on the bridleway and then R (following a large earth bank on your R). Do not take the first kissing gate on your L, but continue ahead and turn L through the next kissing gate by a large gate. Follow the earth track and at a crossing track, turn R on a path that in due course descends on steps and crosses a stream (Castle Bottom on your R). Continue on the path up some steps to a kissing gate by another gate.

3. Turn L along a stony track (with a wooden paling fence on your L). The track narrows, forks L then at a Y junction take the R fork and shortly reach and cross an open space. Turn L on a path descending through holly trees to cross a footbridge. Cross the field diagonally to a wooden gate in its opposite corner, continue half L across the next field to the L of a house and paddock and through a kissing gate in the field corner.

4. Turn R along the road (passing Firgrove Manor on your L); at the T-junction, carefully cross the road, through a gap in the trees and turn L on a path running parallel to the road. In due course keep along the road on its RHS - beware traffic. At the cross roads, go ahead on Up Green and at the T-junction turn R along Chequers Lane (keep along the lane to visit the pubs).

5. Shortly turn L at a metal footpath signpost along a tarmac drive, through a kissing gate and along an enclosed path with woods on your L. At a crossing track, keep along the path on the LH field edge. At the wood corner, turn L along an enclosed path by a green gate with the field on your R. Ignore a footbridge on your L, but at the field corner, cross a footbridge and go through a kissing gate to enter a field. Follow the hedge on your L and shortly at waymark post, turn L along the LH field edge to cross a stile in the field corner. Turn R along the RH edge of two fields, over another stile and a kissing gate. With great care, cross the road and return to Eversley Church.

Walk No 2

THE GOLDEN POT
A FREEHOUSE

Delicious Food
Cask Conditioned Real Ales
Fine Wines
Warm & Welcoming Atmosphere
Monday Evenings Live Music

Visit our website for menus, opening times & entertainment calendar

www.golden-pot.co.uk

Reading Road, Eversley, RG27 0NB
0118 973 2104

Walk No 3   EVERSLEY CROSS & UP GREEN

[4 miles, 2 hours]

1. Start from Eversley Church. Go down the track away from the church and with great care cross the road to the metal footpath signpost about 30 yards to the R. Go through the kissing gate and along the LH field edge, cross a stile and at the corner of the second field, turn L over a stile and along the RH edge of a large field. At a waymark post, turn R to follow the hedge, go through a kissing gate in the corner of a field, over a footbridge and along an enclosed path. At the end of this path (by a green gate on your L), leave the woods on your R and keep ahead on a track for a few yards, then bear L on a footpath across the field (soon with a wire fence on the R). Go through a kissing gate to reach Hollybush Lane.

2. Turn R along the lane; at the T-junction turn L along Chequers Lane (keep along the lane to visit pubs). About 70 yards beyond a white house on your R, turn R at a footpath signpost, through a gate and along an enclosed path to reach the B 3272.

3. Cross this road with great care and go along Fox Lane opposite. Just beyond Fox Cottages and Watmore Farm on the L, turn L at a footpath signpost, through a kissing gate and along an enclosed path; continue ahead past a lake . Turn L through a kissing gate and go between the trees. In 50 yards turn R along the RH field edge and through a kissing gate in the field corner. Follow the enclosed tarmac path, forking R and turn R along Crosby Gardens to the B 3272.

4. Cross this road with great care (using the traffic island) to a byway signpost opposite. Go along this track to pass Firgrove Farm Cottage on your L. Just before the byway signpost, turn R on a path running parallel to Firgrove Road. In due course this path merges with the road - beware traffic. At the cross roads, go ahead on Up Green. At the T-junction, turn L along Up Green (turn R along Chequers Lane for pubs) and just beyond Up Green Farm, look out for a footpath signpost on your R by a gate.

5. Turn R over a stile and along an enclosed path with the farm on your R. Cross two adjacent stiles and a track and follow the RH field edge to a footbridge and stile in the field corner. Turn R and then L along a track (with woods on your R). At a farm gate, take the LH of two stiles and go diagonally half-L across a field to a stile in its LH corner. Go over the next stile just opposite and along the LH field edge, cross a stile in the field corner and then two footbridges with a pond on your R. Go under an electrified wire protected by blue hose, along the LH field edges, under another protected wire and head for the field corner. Go along the L edge of a paddock. At the top corner turn R, then through a gate towards the farm buildings. Just before the farm turn L through a waymarked gap. Turn L on a marked footpath by farm buildings and along the drive to the road. Turn R along the RHS of this road - beware traffic, take extreme care! When it is safe, turn L across the road and return to Eversley Church.

Walk No 4   YATELEY COMMON COUNTRY PARK

[3 ½ miles, 1 ¾ hours]

1. Start from the Royal Oak*, Yateley. Go up Royal Oak Close, turn L past the Police Station, up steps and turn R along the Royal Oak Valley Footpath with a wooden fence on your L. Cross a track and continue on an enclosed path with a wooden fence on your R (crossing a further track). At an open space, cross a track and continue ahead on the path passing The Cricketers on your R. Keep ahead on the LH path through the trees and at a bridleway signpost, turn L along Handford Lane to Cricket Hill Lane.

2. Cross the road carefully, turn R and shortly turn L along track to Yateley Common Country Park. At a T-junction, fork L by a bridleway waymark post towards the edge of Wyndhams Pool (car park on your R). Turn R on the path and follow it round to the pool end and go up the path through the trees. Shortly turn hard R on another path which soon meets a path from the left. Keep ahead passing a waymark post and soon meet a bridleway. Keep ahead and soon go up two shallow steps. Cross a track and continue on to a Y-junction and follow the bridleway bearing L which soon runs close to the A30. Ignore all side turnings and in due course pass a wooden pylon. The path shortly descends some wide steps and in about 80 yards bears L with the fields on your L to arrive at Stroud's Pond.

3. Turn L at the junction and pass Stroud's Pond on your R; continue ahead on the track (can be muddy) and pass Cottage Farm on your L. Turn L at the road, do not enter the farm gate, but take the narrow path through some trees with fields on either side (can be muddy). At T-junction, turn R along a wide track to pass Heathlands Cemetery. Continue along the road, turn L at the T-junction down Stevens Hill to Cricket Hill Lane.

4. Cross the road carefully and into Beaver Lane opposite. Soon fork R, then keep ahead passing Twaingate Cottage. In about 40 yards, turn R along a narrow path (with a wooden fence on your R) and return to the Royal Oak.

* Note. Please ask the Landlord's permission to use the car park. Alternatively use the Yateley Common Country Park (point 2 on the map) car park at Wyndhams Pool.

Walk No 5   FINCHAMPSTEAD & LONGWATER

[4 miles, 2 hours]

1. Start with your back to Finchampstead Church entrance gate. Descend a few yards and at a footpath signpost turn L along Church Lane passing a red brick house on your L. Descend on the track, forking R at Manor Beacon on an enclosed track. Go through a kissing gate and cross the private drive to a kissing gate opposite and follow the enclosed track between fields. At a 4-fingered footpath signpost, go ahead through the posts to an enclosed path on the RH field edge with a wire fence on your L. Pass a wood on your R, continue on an enclosed path, cross a stile and a minor road to a kissing gate opposite by a footpath signpost.

2. Cross the field with a wire fence on your R to another kissing gate. Turn R along the road keeping on the RHS of Fleet Hill (beware of the traffic). In 200 yards cross the road to a lane and a footpath signpost marked the Blackwater Valley Footpath by Vann House (stay on the road for a further 100 yards if you wish to divert to The Tally Ho pub).

3. Pass some paddocks and farm buildings on your R, cross two stiles by farm gates and go along the track on the LH field edge (with Fleet Copse on your L). At the farm gate, cross the stile and bear L to keep along the LH field edge. At the end of the long field, cross two stiles and turn L at a footpath signpost along the path that joins a road (Note the Catherine of Aragon plaque on your L on a footpath signpost).

4. Keep ahead on Longwater Lane through houses; at the T-junction, turn L along the road (go ahead for The Greyhound) and R at the next T-junction. In 50 yards cross the road with care to a footpath signpost opposite. Go up the enclosed stony track/path passing the cricket ground on your L. Keep up the hill passing a seat on your R, ignore the LH turning at a footpath signpost, go ahead through the kissing gate and into churchyard. Leave the churchyard by the RH gate to return to the start.

Walk No 6   FINCHAMPSTEAD RIDGES & MOOR GREEN LAKES

[4 miles, 2 hours]

1. Start from the Horseshoe Lake car park. Go along the track to the Watersports Centre and turn R along the lakeside path. Go through a kissing gate and where the track turns left, keep ahead through another kissing gate, cross the road with care to the footpath signpost and stile opposite. Keep along the LH field edges, over two stiles and through a kissing gate to the road (turn R to visit Ambarrow Court or start from there).

2. Turn L along the road; at Bluebells Farm sign on your R, turn R at the footpath signpost and go along the track. At the Y-junction, fork R on the path with fields on your L and a wood on your R. Fork R at a waymarked post and ascend through the trees. Keep ahead until you reach a T-junction, turn R at the byway signpost along the track and shortly turn L at a footpath signpost and along a track passing a white building on your L. Continue ahead to reach Wellingtonia Avenue (look R to see the giant Sequoia trees lining the Avenue).

3. By the NO PARKING sign, bear L on a permissive footpath and go across the heath. Shortly take the first turning L and descend through the woods (keep ahead to visit Finchampstead Ridges viewpoint). At a large fallen tree on your L, turn L on the permissive path by a waymarked post following a wire fence on the L along a winding path leading to a bar gate (Spout Pond is a few yards along the path to your R). Go through the gap by the bar gate and turn R at a bridleway waymark along the track descending to the road at Moor Green House.

4. Turn R along the road; in 300 yards opposite Pithers Cottage, turn L at the footpath and bridleway signposts along the enclosed Blackwater Valley Footpath (the walk can be started from the car park here). At the Blackwater River, turn L along the riverside path. Do not cross the footbridge over the river, but continue along the riverside. Keep ahead eventually arriving at but not joining Mill Lane. Turn L at the footpath map along a gravel path and over duckboards along the waymarked lakeside path to return to the car park and the walk start.

MAP SHOWING WALK
STARTS 1-12
AND POINTS OF INTEREST

Walk No 7   YATELEY GREEN & BLACKBUSHE

[4 miles - 2 hours]

1. Start from Yateley Town Council Offices. Go L along the B 3272 Reading Road and turn L at The Link; at the T-junction, turn L and shortly fork L on the path across Yateley Green. Cross Hall Lane and follow the footway passing the White Lion on your L and the Dog & Partridge on your R. Go through St Peter's churchyard on a tarmac path to the L of the church. Leave the churchyard and go ahead for 150 yards, turn L along a path that passes beside school playing fields.

2. Cross a road and go along the bridleway opposite. Shortly pass, but do not take the path on your L that leads to the Royal Oak pub. In 50 yards at Oakdene turn R along an enclosed path. At a crossing driveway, keep straight ahead passing The Cricketers and Yateley Baptist Church on your R. Ignore the L fork, but keep ahead on the track through the trees to reach Handford Lane.

3. Cross the road to a bridleway opposite and follow the broad track passing some houses on your R. Continue past the houses straight ahead until the last house, Brackens and take the track at the bridleway signpost through the woods. Shortly after passing under power cables, turn R along the crossing track uphill soon crossing an old road. Keep ahead on the path passing a Gas Pipeline post (can be muddy). Reach the road by the junction with Dungells Lane.

4. Cross the road diagonally R and follow the track opposite leading to a gravel track. Ignore all side turnings, just before an earth bank, turn R on a track through gorse bushes for 20 yards and turn L through the trees. Turn R along an old tarmac track then go over a bank to a road. Turn L along the road (take extreme care with the traffic) to the Anchor Inn on your R.

5. Turn L up Little Vigo and follow the unmade road all the way round to the last house on the R, Oaklands. Keep ahead for 50 yards and turn L through the earth bank to reach an open grassy area. Keep ahead on a path that crosses old airfield hard standings. At the end of an old wide runway, turn R through gorse bushes and bear R along a gravel track. At a T-junction, turn R and immediately L along Monteagle Lane.

6. Pass the Monteagle Arms and continue ahead on Old Monteagle Lane with the school playing fields on your R. Cross School Lane and bear L on a footway and cycleway. At Waitrose, turn R along Monteagle Lane. At the roundabout, bear R and cross Firgrove Road, go through a gap in the wooden barrier opposite and along the enclosed path. After 200 yards, fork R and go through two wooden barriers. At a concrete bollard, go on the path through some trees which leads to a large open grass area and The Link. Turn L and then R to return to the start.

Walk No 8   MINLEY & HAWLEY LAKE

[4 miles, 2 hours]

1. Start from the junction of Minley Road (A 327) and the B 3013. Enter the Defence Lands via a stile. Go ahead on a broad track, after 500 yards at the second ARMED PATROLS notice, do not bear L but keep ahead on a track by jumps. Ignore crossing tracks and descend to cross a tarmac drive and go ahead. Shortly fork R on a track through trees with fields on your L to a sandy track and keep ahead. In due course, cross a concrete road (by large white pyramid bollards) and shortly bear L on a track (bridge on your R). At a Y-junction, keep ahead on the track. Just beyond some overhead pylon cables, meet a crossing bridleway.

2. Ignore the path into the field and turn L after the waymark post along the little used bridleway through the woodland. Continue along L edge of grassland, and in 400 yards pass close to a pylon. After a further 100 yards, at a waymark arrow on a post, bear L and shortly R along the bridleway. Keep ahead ignoring side turnings; in due course pass a metal barrier and along a short length of tarmac road.

3. Cross with care the busy A 327 Minley Road to a bridleway signpost opposite. Go ahead on an earth track through trees, turn L at a waymark post along a track. Pass a metal barrier and turn R along the tarmac road. Pass the Royal Engineers training area and Hawley Lake. Just beyond the Sailing Club the road narrows, pass a metal barrier and take the second turning on the L at a bridleway waymark post, along the gravel track which soon becomes sandy. Turn L at a crossing track and in 40 yards turn R at a waymark post along a track. Keep ahead, ignore side turnings; track ascends and passes other waymark posts to reach the top of the hill.

4. Bear L and in a few yards at a waymark post ahead by a silver birch tree, turn sharp L (not ahead) along a surfaced track. Ignore all side turnings, eventually just before passing the derelict Blackwater Lodge on your L, note the Bronze Age tumulus on your R (unfortunately overgrown). Keep ahead with the Gibraltar Barracks boundary fence on your L, in ½ mile reach and carefully cross the busy Minley Road to return to start.

Crown & Cushion

Minley Road Telephone 01252 545253

Open 12 noon to 11pm (Monday to Saturday) and 10:30pm Sunday

Food served 12 noon to 3pm and 6pm to 9pm

Large Patio area overlooking Cricket Green

Shepherd Neame Best Pub Food Award 2008
Shepherd Neame Pub of The Year 2009

Traditional Country Inn with Meade Banqueting Hall

Walk No 9 FARLEY HILL & LOWER COMMON

[4 ½ miles – 2 ¼ hours]

1. Start from King George V playing field in Castle Road, ¾ mile West of the Fox & Hounds, Farley Hill. Use road side parking or alternatively park at the Fox & Hounds*. From Castle Road walk towards the T-junction and turn L along Church Road. Pass the pub and cross Jouldings Lane. Just beyond Brockendene, turn R at the footpath signpost along the enclosed path. At the fence, turn R along the bottom of the garden and then L along the enclosed path. Turn R over a stile and go along the RH field edge; shortly turn L across the field aiming for a waymark post and then turn R and go along the LH field edge. Cross the stile in the corner of the field, go ahead across the large field aiming for a large pylon.

2. Keep ahead to a stile and footbridge and follow the path through the wood. At the far side of the wood, by a post at its corner, cross the field to a stile in the RH corner. Go along the RH edge of the next field, at the corner of the field by a white house, turn R along a track leading to a road.

3. Turn R along the road and continue on, passing Greenacres Farm signs. At the footpath signpost go ahead on a track, at the next footpath signpost by an iron gate, bear R through a kissing gate and go along the track. Soon look out for a 3-fingered footpath signpost on your R, turn R over a stile (marked The Blackwater Valley Footpath) and across the field to a stile in its opposite LH corner. Cross this and a kissing gate and go along the LH field edge with the Blackwater River on your L. At another kissing gate, turn L at a 3- way footpath signpost along an enclosed path to pass Jouldings Farm and reach a road.

4. Cross the road to a stile and footpath signpost opposite. Go along the LH field edges by the river, crossing a stile and two footbridges to reach a road at Thatchers Ford. Cross the road and stile continuing by the riverside (do not cross the river footbridge). Shortly pass the confluence of the Blackwater and Whitewater Rivers. Keep ahead by the river and in due course at the overhead cables, turn R over a stile by a metal gate and along an enclosed path and over a stile to reach a road.

5. Turn R along the road and L along Sandpit Lane when the T-junction is reached. After 350 yards, look out for a footpath signpost on your L, ascend some steps and go along the LH field edge. At a waymark on a wooden sleeper post, bear R and descend across the field and continue along the road. At the T-junction, turn R and cross Church Road with care to a byway signpost opposite. Bear half L along the drive and track beside Victory Hall and Farley Hill Church. Turn R along Castle Road to return to the start.

*Note. Please ask the Landlord's permission to use the car park.

Walk Nº 9

Map shows a walking route with the following labelled features:
- Farley Hill Church
- Church Road
- Sandpit Lane
- Fox & Hounds
- Jouldings Farm
- Greenacres Farm
- Blackwater River / Ford
- Thatchers Ford
- Numbered waypoints 1–5

John Dollin PRINTING SERVICES LTD

THE COMPLETE PRINT SOLUTION

John Dollin Printing Services Ltd is the **Business Partner** you have been looking for. Whatever your printing requirements, we have the **solution** to produce a **quality product** at a **realistic price**.

- ■ Business Stationery
- ■ Report Covers & Folders
- ■ Annual Report & Accounts
- ■ Personalised Literature
- ■ Newsletters
- ■ Leaflets
- ■ Manuals
- ■ Calendars

For a free quotation contact **Jemma Mayberry** or **Nigel Dollin**:
estimating@johndollinprinting.co.uk   **Telephone: 01256 892969**

Walk No 10 FINCHAMPSTEAD & BLACKWATER RIVER

[4 ½ miles, 2 ¼ hours]

1. Start from Finchampstead Church * (or see end of paragraph 3). Enter the churchyard and pass to the R of the church tower, descend on the path, through a kissing gate and along the enclosed path. In 100 yards at a 3-fingered signpost, turn R along an enclosed path; just beyond a signpost, turn L and then R. At a T-junction by white buildings, turn L and soon go through a kissing gate, along a drive to reach a road.

2. Turn L, and just before the garage cross the busy road with care (watch traffic), at a signpost go over a stile and along an enclosed path. At a 3-fingered signpost (Catherine of Aragon plaque just to the L) turn R along a track. At another 3-fingered signpost, keep ahead, and soon cross a wooden footbridge. Shortly turn L through a kissing gate along a gravel path (Blackwater Valley Footpath) along the RH edge of a large field. In due course reach and carefully cross the busy road to a kissing gate opposite on your R.

3. Continue along the enclosed gravel path on the RH side of gravel workings. Turn L along the path that follows the Blackwater River. Pass but do not cross a gravel extraction bridge on your R. Eventually cross a small wooden footbridge (not over the Blackwater) and turn L along the RH of two enclosed tracks (the other one is a bridleway). Pass Moor Green Lakes on your R, go over a wooden bridge and keep along the RH track. In due course reach a car park by the road.
* Note. The walk can be started from here (please be aware that this car park is locked in the evening).

4. Turn L along the road and in 150 yards, turn R along Dell Road. The road winds and ascends onto the Finchampstead Ridges to reach and cross a busy road to a bridleway signpost opposite.

5. Go along the bridleway. Ignore the LH turn at the top of the hill (just before Wick Hill House) and keep ahead. The bridleway narrows at Tudor Cottage (on your L), the track descends and eventually passes through a wooden barrier on to a surfaced road. Keep ahead, shortly the road bears R, fork L on an earth track that soon ascends. At Silver Wood on your R, turn L at a signpost by a blue gate and in a few yards at Warren Crest Farm, fork R along a wide enclosed track. Go through a gap and keep ahead on an enclosed path, then through a kissing gate to reach a road.

6. Cross with care the busy road to the signpost and climb the stile opposite. Bear half L diagonally across the field to its opposite LH corner. Turn R up the road (watch for traffic) and pass the Queens Oak pub and return to the Church (there is a good footpath map located between the pub and the church).

Walk No 11   COVE BROOK & HAWLEY COMMON

[5 ½ miles, 2 ¾ hours]

1. Start from the car park by the bridge over Cove Brook near to Highfield Path. Go along Highfield Path, at the end of the road enter the enclosed path leading to Holly Road. Shortly turn L along a tarmac track, under the railway bridge and turn L along the path at the base of the embankment. At the Five Arch Bridge, turn R along the path on the RHS of Cove Brook.

2. Shortly cross West Heath Road and continue on the footpath opposite on the RHS of Cove Brook. Cross the footbridge over Cove Brook, turn R across a large grass area. Cross back over Cove Brook by the footbridge, turn L along a gravel path on the RHS of Cove Brook. Pass but do not cross another footbridge over Cove Brook and continue on the gravel path on the RHS of Cove Brook.

3. Cross a road and continue on the gravel path opposite. Pass but do not cross a further footbridge over Cove Brook and continue on the gravel brookside footpath. Go under the M3 bridge and keep ahead to reach Hawley Lane.

4. Turn L along the footway and just before the roundabout, cross with great care Hawley Road. Turn L along the footway and shortly pass The New Inn. Keep ahead beyond Ashbury Drive and soon pass Fernhill Lane on your L (The walk can be shortened by turning L up Fernhill Lane). Soon leave the busy Hawley Road and bear R on a tarmac track passing cottages and go along the old road. Go through a gap and keep on the old road that soon merges with Hawley Road. Go ahead on the footway to reach Hawley Lodge on your R.

5. Cross the busy Hawley Road with great care, to the field gate opposite. Cross the metal stile, turn L on the path across the field (with a fence on your R) to cross another metal stile to reach Fernhill Lane. Turn R up Fernhill Lane (no footway for 700 yards); ignore all side turnings and in due course descend to Fernhill Road.

6. Cross the road with great care, turn R on the footway up the hill and just beyond Abercorn House, turn L along Woodlands Walk. At Hawley Place Gardens, pass a metal gate and keep ahead on a wide bridleway. Ignore all side turnings and in just over ½ mile, fork R off the track to pass Hawley Lake on your R. Go ahead on a tarmac road crossing a brick parapet bridge over the outlet stream of Hawley Lake. Shortly fork L at a Y-junction and on reaching a wooden fence on your L, go through a barrier and along a wide gravel meandering path (buildings on your R). Turn L along a concrete road to reach Sandy Lane.

7. Cross the road with care to The Potteries opposite; shortly turn R on a path through trees and pass under the M3 via a narrow bridge. Go ahead along Woodlands Road to reach and carefully cross Minley Road. Turn L along the footway and enter St John's churchyard. Leave it by the lychgate and take the enclosed church path opposite.

8. Turn R along Minley Road and go clockwise past the roundabout. Just before the railway bridge, turn L along the footpath behind the houses. Go over the Five Arch Bridge and soon turn R under the railway bridge and R again along Holly Road and Highfield Path to return to the start.

Walk No 12   BLACKWATER RIVER & BASINGSTOKE CANAL

[5 miles, 2 ½ hours]

1. Start from Carrington Recreation car park *(or see end of paragraph 4), Ash Vale (Note. Car park closes at dusk). Go along the tarmac drive (with the large green on your L), past the red and white barrier, turn L and carefully cross Lysons Avenue. Turn R and then L onto a tarmac path to North Camp Station level crossing. Keep ahead on the road and in a few yards at a Blackwater Valley Path signpost, turn R across the road and under a bridge (beside the Blackwater River).

2. Cross over Lynchford Lane, keep ahead and soon turn R at a Blackwater Valley Path North signpost. Go along a gravel path beside the busy Blackwater Valley Road, pass a gasometer on your R, over a railway bridge and descend on a path that passes under the road (beside the Blackwater River). Shortly cross a footbridge over the Blackwater River and go through Gerry's Copse. Re-cross the river on a footbridge, turn L along the track. Cross another footbridge over the river and in due course go up a slope to Coleford Bridge Road.

3. Turn R at a Blackwater Valley Path North signpost, over the bridge, turn R down some steps and turn R along a broad tarmac track going under the bridge. Pass the Quays sign on your R, fork R down a path to the R of a metal gate and follow the path beside the Blackwater River. Cross a footbridge and turn R along the track, go under the railway bridge, pass under a concrete bridge and turn R over another footbridge. Do NOT turn L through a gate along the Blackwater Valley Path, but go ahead and turn L on an enclosed bridleway, The Hatches, passing between two lakes. Carefully go over the railway level crossing to reach the road.

4. Go ahead on The Hatches, turn R at Cross Lane and follow The Hatches to pass Frimley Green on your L (Rose & Thistle opposite). Cross Sturt Road with care, turn R to pass the pub and the publlc toilets and go under the railway bridge. Pass St Andrews Church and turn L into Frimley Lodge Park. *Note. The walk can be started from here.

Keep along the track with the car park on your L. Pass on your R a signpost to the Pavilion and Canal North. Follow the track to the R of the Pavilion with a sports field on your R. At the crossing of a tarmac road, turn L and arrive at the Frimley Lodge Park Miniature Railway wooden shed. Turn L and reach the Basingstoke Canal towpath.

5. Turn R along the towpath and in due course pass the Basingstoke Canal Centre (on opposite bank), under Mytchett Place Road bridge and next Mytchett Lake Road bridge to pass Mytchett Lake. Soon pass under the railway bridge and turn R off the towpath down a short track to reach the road. Turn L along Frimley Road and in 250 yards carefully cross the road and turn R into Carrington Lane to return to the start.

POINTS OF INTEREST
Eversley

Castle Bottom is close to the site of former cottages on Eversley Common, but little trace of them remains. It is a surprisingly isolated hollow of ancient heathland that is now a Nature Reserve and is close to Blackbushe Airfield. Traces of a low round tumulus were said to be obliterated by wartime airfield works. It was on the main dyke boundary of Crondall Manor confirmed by King Edgar in 975. A bank along the parish boundary to the present A30 was made by the Militia encamped locally in 1803.

(Walk No 2)

The Church of Blessed Mary the Virgin There was a church on the site by 1294. The chancel was built about 1500; in 1724 the whole church, west of the chancel screen, was re-built by John James. The tower was completed in 1736. In 1876 the church was restored as a memorial to Charles Kingsley, rector from 1844 until his death in 1875. He was a social reformer, naturalist, author of The Water-Babies, but probably most importantly a simple, well-loved, parish priest. He was buried beside the avenue of Irish yews he planted in the churchyard.

(Walk Nos 1, 2 & 3)

Cross Green Eversley's ancient origins are suggested by the village sign erected on the green commemorating Queen Elizabeth's Silver Jubilee in 1975. Eversley's name may be derived from E for Leigh or field of the wild boar. It is one of the few remaining records of the existence of wild boars in England. The cricket ground on the green is the venue of an annual benefit match with Hampshire. Close to the pond are the remains of a unusual spigot mortar, erected during the 1940 defence works.

(Walk No 3)

Firgrove Manor Wadham Wyndham prospered in the service of the South Sea Company and this, together with a dowry of £8000 on marrying his cousin Catherine, enabled him early in the 18th century to build Firgrove Manor - possibly by John James. It may occupy the site of an earlier building or monastery. The Wyndhams were a Saxon family of nobility from Norfolk. They were one of the two leading families in Yateley and strong supporters of the Jacobites in southern England. Wadham Wyndham was a well-known amateur coachman.

(Walk Nos 2 & 3)

New Mill dates from 1577 when it replaced an earlier mill destroyed by fire. The Domesday Book records two mills in the vicinity. For over three hundred years New Mill was owned by the St John family who rented it to the Spencers. A later tenant, Mr Westcott, added the lock bridge and started a saw mill. Local farmers brought corn to the mill for grinding until early in the 20th century. New Mill is a listed building and has been a restaurant since 1972. The water wheel and corn grinding equipment are still in working order.

(Walk No 1)

Warbrook House was built in 1724 by the architect John James for himself. Despite recent additions, the period building has survived virtually intact. The grounds were laid out using the principles of Dezallier d'Argentville; James translated the French Treatise. The West front of Warbrook House has a breath-taking view down the tree-lined canal which exemplifies his mastery of landscaping. James was born in 1672 at Stratfield Turgis, educated at Basingstoke and apprenticed to Matthew Bankes, the King's Carpenter. He became an architect and, as a colleague of Christopher Wren, was involved in the completion of St Paul's Cathedral where he was surveyor to the fabric. He designed many other buildings in London after the Great Fire in 1666 and also a number of buildings in Hampshire. His achievements are recorded on a memorial tablet in Eversley Church.

(Walk No 1)

The Welsh Drive is an old drovers' road used to take cattle from Wales and the West Country to London. This stopped when the railways developed. An annual fair was held on 8 November at Blackwater. The Welsh Drive passes close to Cudbury Clump a Bronze Age burial barrow.

(Walk Nos 1 & 2)

Finchampstead

Catherine of Aragon In 1501 Prince Arthur, eldest son of Henry VII, started out from Windsor Castle to meet his fiancee Catherine of Aragon. He was met at Finchampstead by her guardians. The meeting spot is marked by a plaque. Against royal Spanish custom, Prince Henry rode on to meet her at Dogmersfield. A dance was held there in the evening. (Walk Nos 5 & 10)

Finchampstead Ridges is National Trust property and provides a fine viewpoint across the Blackwater Valley and parts of Berkshire, Hampshire and Surrey. Just to the north, the London to Silchester Roman Road called the Devil's Highway crosses Simons Wood. Wellingtonia Avenue is an outstanding half-mile avenue of hundred Sequoia trees, planted in 1863 in memory of the Duke of Wellington. (Walk Nos 6 & 10)

Moor Green Lakes are a nature reserve restored from former gravel pits. Habitats have been created for a wide variety of birds which can be seen from the Blackwater Valley Footpath.

(Walks Nos 6 & 10)

Parish Church of St James retains the walls of the original church built about the time of the Norman Conquest. The Normans elaborated the simple Saxon church to its more or less present form in about 1150. The font is the original - credited 1030. About 1375 a small chapel was added on the north side removing part of the Norman wall. The chapel was extended about 1475 and a corner entrance constructed in 1590. The red brick tower built in 1720 has six bells dating from 1792. A list of rectors from 1299 is in the 19th century porch. (Walk Nos 5 & 10)

Hawley

Crown & Cushion has associations with Colonel Thomas Blood who lived at Minley Warren. In 1671 he nearly succeeded in stealing the Crown Jewels from the Tower of London. Although he escaped, he was later arrested whilst imbibing in the Crown & Cushion. This was commemorated by a topiary in front of the pub cut in the shape of a crown on a cushion, sadly no longer trimmed. Blood was granted a Royal Pardon and an estate in Ireland worth £500 a year. Who said crime does not pay!

(Walk No 8)

Hawley Lake in Hawley Common is a popular walking, sailing and fishing area. The Common was part of the Minley Manor grounds owned by the Currie family, local benefactors who gave ground for the cricket pavilion by Hawley Green and later for the Hawley War Memorial Hall. The lake and surrounding common are now used by the Royal Engineers as a training area and walkers should keep to the paths. (Walk Nos 8 & 11)

Minley Manor was rebuilt in 1858-60 for Raikes Currie a London Banker and MP for Northampton. The architect was Henry Clutton and the design was said to be inspired by the Chateau de Blois. The Manor was enlarged later and remained with the Currie family until it was purchased by the War Office in 1936. Since 1971 it has been used by the Royal Engineers from the adjacent Gibraltar Barracks.

(Walk No 8)

Sandhurst

Ambarrow Court was built in 1885 for Colonel Harvey from designs by the architect F Ravenscroft; it was surrounded by over 21 acres of woodland. On his widow's death, it was offered for sale in 1932 by Messrs Nicholas of Reading for use as a school, nursing home or institution. In Autumn 1940 it was requisitioned as an outstation of Radio Department, Royal Aircraft Establishment (RAE) following the bombing of RAE Farnborough in August 1940. The house was then empty, but it contained much German literature which lends credence to the rumours that it had been used for the interrogation of enemy agents. After it was relinquished by the RAE in 1969, it became derelict and the house was demolished. The weather-cock was preserved on a building in the RAE. The grounds, once a "secret garden", are now open to the public as is adjacent Ambarrow Hill. (Walk No 6)

Yateley

Blackbushe airfield was built on common land in the Second World War and was known as RAF Hartford Bridge. It was crossed by the Welsh Drive and the road over the common to Vigo Lane which has never been re-opened. One runway crossed the A30 and traffic was diverted onto the Fleet Road. The airfield was first used by Aerodynamics Flight, Royal Aircraft Establishment testing gliders later used at D-Day. A variety of operational squadrons used the airfield including: RCAF Tomahawks, RAF photographic reconnaissance Spitfires, RAF and Free French Boston bombers and Polish Mosquitoes. The airfield had FIDO - a fog dispersal system. There is a memorial plaque at the airfield honouring aircrew lost in action. (Walk No 7)

St Peter's Parish Church is built on the site of a Saxon church said to have been burnt down about 750. The earliest record of the church is in the Domesday Book 1080. There is a roll of incumbents back to 1226. The north wall from behind the wooden font to the organ is Saxon and was extended to its present length in about 1100. The chancel was completed about 1220 and the wooden tower about 1500. The church was burnt down in 1979 leaving only the walls, charred timbers of the tower and cracked bells - the oldest cast in 1557. The church was re-built by 1981. The chancel became the chapel and contains the 13th century font; the 1600 clock was restored. (Walk No 7)

Yateley Common Country Park is one of the few remaining heathlands in North East Hampshire. It was originally cleared of forest in the Bronze Age for crops and livestock. The poor soil was soon exhausted and colonised by plants such as heather and gorse. For hundreds of years it was kept open by commoners cutting fuel and turf and by continuous grazing. As this declined, birch and pine invaded the Common. This has been reversed by the Country Park Rangers careful management. Stroud Pond was recorded in the Domesday Book as a fish pond; stakes to prevent poaching have been traced. Wyndham's Pool is named after a local family. (Walk No 4)

Blackwater Valley Footpath

Blackwater River has its source in Rowhill Nature Reserve between Aldershot and Farnham. The river forms the county boundaries between Hampshire, Surrey and Berkshire. A continuous footpath follows the course of Blackwater River from its source to its confluence with the River Loddon. Many of the circular walks described in this book follow sections of the Blackwater Valley Footpath or give a vista across the Blackwater Valley. There is also a footpath beside Cove Brook, a tributary of the Blackwater, which unfortunately does not connect with it.

Thatchers Ford is where the Roman Road (known as the Devil's Highway) crossed the Blackwater River. (Walk No 9)